THE GREAT STORY

MADONNA DEL GRANDUCA, by RAPHAEL
Courtesy of David Ashley, Inc.

The Great Story

From the Authorized
King James Version of the Bible, N.T. Gospels

HARCOURT, BRACE AND COMPANY
NEW YORK

first edition

PRINTED IN THE UNITED STATES OF AMERICA
BY DUENEWALD PRINTING CORPORATION, NEW YORK
COMPOSITION AND BINDING BY QUINN & BODEN COMPANY, INC.
RAHWAY, NEW JERSEY

LIST OF ILLUSTRATIONS

THE GREAT STORY

I

NOW the birth of Jesus Christ was on this wise: The angel Gabriel was sent from God unto a city of Galilee, named Nazareth, to a virgin espoused to a man whose name was Joseph, of the house of David; and the virgin's name was Mary. And the angel came in unto her and said:

3

"Hail, thou that art highly favoured, the Lord is with thee. Blessed art thou among women!"

When she saw him, she was troubled at his saying, and cast in her mind what manner of salutation this should be. And the angel said unto her:

"Fear not, Mary, for thou hast found favour with God. And behold thou shalt bring forth a son, and shalt call his name Jesus. He shall be great, and shall be called the Son of the Highest, and the Lord God shall give unto him the throne of his father David. And he shall reign over the house of Jacob for ever; and of his kingdom there shall be no end."

Then said Mary unto the angel, "How shall this be?" And the angel answered and said unto her:

"The Holy Ghost shall come upon thee, and the power of the Highest shall overshadow thee. Therefore also that holy thing which shall be born of thee shall be called the Son of God."

It came to pass in those days that there went out a decree from Caesar Augustus that all the world should be taxed, and all went to be taxed, every one into his own city. Joseph also went up from Galilee, out of the city of Nazareth, into Judaea, unto the city of David which is called Bethlehem (because he was of the house and lineage of David) to be taxed with Mary, his espoused wife, being great with child. While they were there the days were accomplished that she should be delivered. And she brought forth her firstborn son, and wrapped him in swaddling clothes, and laid him in a manger; because there was no room for them in the inn.

And there were in the same country shepherds abiding in the field, keeping watch over their flock by night. And lo, the angel of the Lord came upon them, and the glory of the Lord shone round about them, and they were sore afraid. And the angel said unto them:

"Fear not, for behold I bring you good tidings of great joy, which shall be to all people. For unto you is born this day in the city of David a Saviour, which is Christ the Lord. And this shall be a sign unto you: Ye shall find the babe wrapped in swaddling clothes, lying in a manger."

And suddenly there was with the angel a multitude of the heavenly host praising God and saying:

"Glory to God in the highest, and on earth peace, good will toward men."

It came to pass, as the angels were gone away from them into heaven, the shepherds said one to another, "Let us now go even unto Bethlehem, and see this thing which is come to pass, which the Lord hath made known unto us." And they came with haste, and found Mary and Joseph, and the babe lying in a manger. When they had seen it, they made known abroad the saying which was told them concerning this child. And all they that heard it wondered at those things which were told them by the shepherds. But Mary kept all these things, and pondered them in her heart. And the shepherds returned, glorifying and praising God for all the things that they had heard and seen, as it was told unto them.

When eight days were accomplished, the child's name was called Jesus. And they brought him to

Jerusalem to present him to the Lord.

Behold there was a man in Jerusalem whose name was Simeon; and the same man was just and devout, waiting for the consolation of Israel, and the Holy Ghost was upon him. It was revealed unto him by the Holy Ghost that he should not see death before he had seen the Lord's Christ. And he came by the Spirit into the temple; and when the parents brought in the child Jesus, then took he him up in his arms and blessed God and said:

"Lord, now lettest thou thy servant depart in peace, according to thy word: for mine eyes have seen thy salvation which thou hast prepared before the face of all people, a light to lighten the Gentiles, and the glory of thy people Israel."

Joseph and his mother marvelled at those things which were spoken of him. And Simeon blessed them and said unto Mary his mother, "Behold, this child is set for the fall and rising again of many in Israel."

Now when Jesus was born in Bethlehem of Judaea, in the days of Herod the king, behold there came

ADORATION OF THE SHEPHERDS, by *GHIRLANDAIO*
(1449-1494)
The original is in the Church of the Holy Trinity, Florence.
Courtesy of Rudolph Lesch Fine Arts, Inc.

wise men from the east to Jerusalem, saying: "Where is he that is born King of Jews? For we have seen his star in the east, and are come to worship him."

When Herod the king had heard these things, he was troubled and all Jerusalem with him. And when he had gathered all the chief priests and scribes of the people together, he demanded of them where Christ should be born. They said unto him:

"In Bethlehem of Judaea. For thus it is written by the prophet: 'And thou Bethlehem, in the land of Juda, art not the least among the princes of Juda. For out of thee shall come a Governor that shall rule my people Israel.'"

Then Herod, when he had privily called the wise men, enquired of them diligently what time the star appeared. And he sent them to Bethlehem, and said, "Go and search diligently for the young child; and when ye have found him, bring me word again, that I may come and worship him also."

When they had heard the king, they departed. And lo, the star which they saw in the east went before

ADORATION OF THE MAGI, by *GENTILE DA FABRIANO*
(c. 1370-c. 1450)
The original is in the Uffizi, Florence.
Courtesy of Rudolph *Lesch Fine Arts*, Inc.

them till it came and stood over where the young child was. When they saw the star, they rejoiced with exceeding great joy. And when they were come into the house, they saw the young child with Mary his mother, and fell down and worshipped him. When they had opened their treasures, they presented unto him gifts: gold, and frankincense, and myrrh. And being warned of God in a dream that they should not return to Herod, they departed into their own country another way.

When they were departed, behold the angel of the Lord appeareth to Joseph in a dream, saying:

"Arise, and take the young child and his mother and flee into Egypt, and be thou there until I bring thee word; for Herod will seek the young child to destroy him."

When he arose, he took the young child and his mother by night and departed into Egypt, and was there until the death of Herod, that it might be fulfilled which was spoken of the Lord by the prophet, saying, "Out of Egypt have I called my son." Then

Herod, when he saw that he was mocked of the wise men, was exceeding wroth, and sent forth and slew all the children that were in Bethlehem and in all the coasts thereof, from two years old and under, according to the time which he had diligently inquired of the wise men.

But when Herod was dead, behold an angel of the Lord appeareth in a dream to Joseph in Egypt, saying, "Arise, and take the young child and his mother and go into the land of Israel, for they are dead which sought the young child's life." And he arose and took the young child and his mother and came into the land of Israel. But when he heard that Archelaus did reign in Judaea in the room of his father Herod, he was afraid to go thither. Notwithstanding, being warned of God in a dream, he turned aside into the parts of Galilee. And he came and dwelt in Nazareth.

And the child grew and waxed strong in spirit, filled with wisdom; and the grace of God was upon him.

Now his parents went to Jerusalem every year at

the feast of the passover. When he was twelve years old, they went up to Jerusalem after the custom of the feast. And when they had fulfilled the days, as they returned, the child Jesus tarried behind in Jerusalem; and Joseph and his mother knew not of it. But they, supposing him to have been in the company, went a day's journey; and they sought him among their kinsfolk and acquaintance. When they found him not, they turned back again to Jerusalem, seeking him.

It came to pass that after three days they found him in the temple, sitting in the midst of the doctors, both hearing them and asking them questions. And all that heard him were astonished at his understanding and answers. When they saw him, they were amazed, and his mother said unto him: "Son, why hast thou thus dealt with us? Behold thy father and I have sought thee sorrowing."

He said unto them, "How is it that ye sought me? Wist ye not that I must be about my Father's business?" and they understood not the saying which he

FLIGHT INTO EGYPT, by *GENTILE DA FABRIANO*
(c. 1370-c. 1450)
The original is in the Uffizi, Florence.
Courtesy of Rudolph Lesch Fine Arts, Inc.

spake unto them. And he went down with them, and came to Nazareth, and was subject unto them. But his mother kept all these sayings in her heart.

And Jesus increased in wisdom and stature and in favour with God and man.

II

IN those days came John the Baptist, preaching in the wilderness of Judaea and saying, "Repent ye, for the kingdom of heaven is at hand." The same John had his raiment of camel's hair, and a leathern girdle about his loins, and his meat was locusts and wild honey. Then went out to him Jerusalem, and all Judaea, and all the region round about Jordan, and were baptized of him in Jordan, confessing their sins. And he said unto them:

"I indeed baptize you with water unto repentance. But he that cometh after me is mightier than I, whose shoes I am not worthy to bear. He shall baptize you with the Holy Ghost and with fire."

Then cometh Jesus, being about thirty years of age, from Galilee to Jordan unto John, to be baptized of him. But John forbad him, saying, "I have need to be baptized of thee, and comest thou to me?"

Jesus answering said unto him, "Suffer it to be so now. For thus it becometh us to fulfil all righteousness." Then he suffered him.

Jesus, when he was baptized, went up straightway out of the water. And lo, the heavens were opened unto him, and he saw the Spirit of God descending like a dove, and lighting upon him. And lo, a voice from heaven saying, "This is my beloved Son, in whom I am well pleased."

Jesus, being full of the Holy Ghost, returned from Jordan and was led by the Spirit into the wilderness, being forty days tempted of the devil. In those days he did eat nothing, and when they were ended, he afterward hungered.

And the devil said unto him, "If thou be the Son of God, command this stone that it be made bread."

Jesus answered him, saying, "It is written that man shall not live by bread alone, but by every word of God."

And the devil, taking him up into an high mountain, shewed unto him all the kingdoms of the world in a moment of time. And the devil said únto him: "All this power will I give thee and the glory of them. For that is delivered unto me, and to whomsoever I will I give it. If thou therefore wilt worship me, all shall be thine."

Jesus answered and said unto him: "Get thee behind me, Satan. For it is written, 'Thou shalt worship the Lord thy God and him only shalt thou serve.' "

And he brought him to Jerusalem, and set him on a pinnacle of the temple, and said unto him: "If thou be the Son of God, cast thyself down from hence. For it is written, 'He shall give his angels charge over thee, to keep thee. And in their hands they shall bear thee up lest at any time thou dash thy foot against a stone.' "

Jesus answering said unto him, "It is said, 'Thou shalt not tempt the Lord thy God.' "

When the devil had ended all the temptation, he departed from him for a season. And Jesus returned in the power of the Spirit into Galilee. And there went out a fame of him through all the region round about, and he taught in their synagogues, being glorified of all.

And he came to Nazareth, where he had been brought up, and, as his custom was, he went into the synagogue on the sabbath day and stood up for to read. And there was delivered unto him the book of the prophet Esaias, and when he had opened the book, he found the place where it was written:

"The Spirit of the Lord is upon me, because he hath anointed me to preach the gospel to the poor. He hath sent me to heal the brokenhearted, to preach deliverance to the captives and recovering of sight to the blind, to set at liberty them that are bruised, to preach the acceptable year of the Lord."

And he closed the book, and he gave it again to the minister, and sat down, and the eyes of all them that were in the synagogue were fastened on him. And he began to say unto them, "This day is the scripture fulfilled in your ears." And all bare him witness, and wondered at the gracious words which

HEAD OF CHRIST, attributed to *LEONARDO DA VINCI*
(1452-1519)
The original is in the Pinacoteca di Brera, Milan.
Courtesy of David Ashley, Inc.

proceeded out of his mouth, and they said, "Is not this Joseph's son?"

He said unto them: "Ye will surely say unto me this proverb: 'Physician, heal thyself. Whatsoever we have heard done in Capernaum, do also here in thy country.'" And he said, "Verily I say unto you, no prophet is accepted in his own country."

All they in the synagogue, when they heard these things, were filled with wrath, and rose up and thrust him out of the city, and led him unto the brow of the hill whereon their city was built, that they might cast him down headlong. But he, passing through the midst of them, went his way, and came down to Capernaum, a city of Galilee, and taught them on the sabbath days. And they were astonished at his doctrine, for his word was with power.

It came to pass that as the people pressed upon him to hear the word of God, he stood by the lake of Gennesaret, and saw two ships standing by the lake. But the fishermen were gone out of them and were washing their nets. He entered into one of the ships, which was Simon's, and prayed him that he would thrust out a little from the land. And he sat down and taught the people out of the ship.

Now when he had left speaking, he said unto Simon, "Launch out into the deep and let down your nets for a draught." Simon answering said unto him: "Master, we have toiled all the night and have taken nothing. Nevertheless at thy word I will let down the net." When they had this done, they inclosed a great multitude of fishes and their net brake. And they beckoned unto their partners, which were in the other ship, that they should come and help them, and they came and filled both ships, so that they began to sink.

When Simon Peter saw it, he fell down at Jesus' knees, saying, "Depart from me, for I am a sinful man, O Lord." For he was astonished, and all that were with him, at the draught of the fishes which they had taken. And so was also James, and John, the sons of Zebedee, which were partners with Simon. Jesus said unto Simon, "Fear not. From henceforth thou shalt catch men." And when they had brought their ships to land, they forsook all and followed him.

There was a marriage in Cana of Galilee, and the mother of Jesus was there. And both Jesus was called, and his disciples, to the marriage. When they wanted wine, the mother of Jesus saith unto him, "They have no wine." And there were set there six waterpots of stone, after the manner of the purifying of the Jews, containing two or three firkins apiece. Jesus saith unto them, "Fill the waterpots with water." And they filled them up to the brim. He saith unto them, "Draw out now, and bear unto the governor of the feast." And they bare it.

When the ruler of the feast had tasted the water that was made wine and knew not whence it was (but the servants which drew the water knew), the governor of the feast called the bridegroom and saith unto him: "Every man at the beginning doth set forth good wine, and when men have well drunk, then that which is worse. But thou hast kept the good wine until now."

CHRIST AND THE SONS OF ZEBEDEE, by MARCO BASAITI
(?-1521)
The original is in the Academy, Venice.
Courtesy of Rudolph Lesch Fine Arts, Inc.

After this he went down to Capernaum, he, and his mother, and his brethren, and his disciples. And straightway on the sabbath day he entered into the synagogue and taught. And there was in their synagogue a man with an unclean spirit, and he cried out, saying:

"Let us alone. What have we to do with thee, thou Jesus of Nazareth? Art thou come to destroy us? I know thee who thou art, the Holy One of God."

Jesus rebuked him, saying, "Hold thy peace and come out of him." And when the unclean spirit had torn him and cried with a loud voice, he came out of him. And they were all amazed, insomuch that they questioned among themselves, saying: "What thing is this? For with authority commandeth he even the unclean spirits and they do obey him." And immediately his fame spread abroad throughout all the region round about Galilee.

When they were come out of the synagogue, they entered into the house of Simon and Andrew, with James and John. At even, when the sun did set, they brought unto him all that were diseased and them that were possessed with devils. And all the city was gathered together at the door, and he healed many that were sick of divers diseases and cast out many devils, and suffered not the devils to speak, because they knew him.

There was a certain nobleman whose son was sick at Capernaum. When he heard that Jesus was come out of Judaea into Galilee, he went unto him and besought him that he would come down and heal his son, for he was at the point of death. Then said Jesus unto him, "Except ye see signs and wonders, ye will not believe." The nobleman saith unto him, "Sir, come down ere my child die." Jesus saith unto him, "Go thy way. Thy son liveth." And the man believed the word that Jesus had spoken unto him and he went his way.

As he was now going down, his servants met him and told him, saying, "Thy son liveth." Then enquired he of them the hour when he began to amend. They said unto him, "Yesterday at the seventh hour the fever left him." So the father knew that it was at the same hour in the which Jesus said unto him, "Thy son liveth," and himself believed, and his whole house.

III

JESUS went about all Galilee, teaching in their synagogues, and preaching the gospel of the kingdom, and healing all manner of sickness and all manner of disease among the people, and his fame went throughout all Syria. And they brought unto him all sick people that were taken with divers diseases and torments, and those which were possessed with devils, and those which were lunatick, and those that had the palsy; and he healed them.

There followed him great multitudes of people from Galilee, and from Decapolis, and from Jerusalem, and from Judaea, and from beyond Jordan. And seeing the multitudes, he went up into a mountain. And when he was set, his disciples came unto him, and he opened his mouth and taught them, saying:

"Blessed are the poor in spirit, for theirs is the kingdom of heaven.

"Blessed are they that mourn, for they shall be comforted.

"Blessed are the meek, for they shall inherit the earth.

"Blessed are they which do hunger and thirst after righteousness, for they shall be filled.

"Blessed are the merciful, for they shall obtain mercy.

"Blessed are the pure in heart, for they shall see God.

"Blessed are the peacemakers, for they shall be called the children of God.

"Blessed are they which are persecuted for righteousness' sake, for theirs is the kingdom of heaven.

"Blessed are ye, when men shall revile you, and persecute you, and shall say all manner of evil against you falsely, for my sake. Rejoice and be exceeding glad, for great is your reward in heaven. For so persecuted they the prophets which were before you.

"Ye are the light of the world. A city that is set on an hill cannot be hid. Neither do men light a candle and put it under a bushel, but on a candle-stick, and it giveth light unto all that are in the house. Let your light so shine before men that they may see your good works and glorify your Father which is in heaven.

"Think not that I am come to destroy the law or the prophets. I am not come to destroy, but to fulfil.

"Ye have heard that it hath been said, 'Thou shalt love thy neighbour and hate thine enemy.' But I say unto you, love your enemies, bless them that curse you, do good to them that hate you, and pray for them which despitefully use you and persecute you, that ye may be the children of your Father which is in heaven. For he maketh his sun to rise on the evil and on the good, and sendeth rain on the just and on the unjust.

"And when thou prayest, thou shalt not be as the hypocrites are. For they love to pray standing in the synagogues and in the corners of the streets, that they may be seen of men. Verily I say unto you, they have their reward. But thou, when thou prayest, enter into thy closet, and when thou hast shut thy door, pray to thy Father which is in secret. And thy Father which seeth in secret shall reward thee openly. After this manner therefore pray ye:

"Our Father which art in heaven, hallowed be thy name. Thy kingdom come. Thy will be done in earth as it is in heaven. Give us this day our daily bread, and forgive us our debts as we forgive our debtors. And lead us not into temptation, but deliver us from evil. For thine is the kingdom, and the power, and the glory, for ever. Amen.

"Lay not up for yourselves treasures upon earth, where moth and rust doth corrupt, and where thieves break through and steal. But lay up for yourselves treasures in heaven, where neither moth nor rust doth corrupt, and where thieves do not break through nor steal. For where your treasure is, there will your heart be also.

"No man can serve two masters. For either he will hate the one and love the other, or else he will hold to the one and despise the other. Ye cannot serve

SUFFER THE LITTLE CHILDREN, by *CHRISTIAN VOGEL*
(1759-1816)
The original is in the Gallery of Modern Art, Florence.
Courtesy of Rudolph Lesch Fine Arts, Inc.

God and mammon.

"Therefore I say unto you, take no thought for your life, what ye shall eat or what ye shall drink, nor yet for your body, what ye shall put on. Is not the life more than meat, and the body than raiment? Behold the fowls of the air, for they sow not, neither do they reap, nor gather into barns. Yet your heavenly Father feedeth them. Are ye not much better than they?

"And why take ye thought for raiment? Consider the lilies of the field, how they grow. They toil not, neither do they spin. And yet I say unto you that even Solomon in all his glory was not arrayed like one of these. Wherefore, if God so clothe the grass of the field, which today is and tomorrow is cast into the oven, shall he not much more clothe you, O ye of little faith?

"Therefore take no thought, saying, 'What shall we eat?' or, 'What shall we drink?' or, 'Wherewithal shall we be clothed?' For your heavenly Father knoweth that ye have need of all these things. But seek ye first the kingdom of God and his righteousness, and all these things shall be added unto you. Take therefore no thought for the morrow. For the morrow shall take thought for the things of itself. Sufficient unto the day is the evil thereof.

"Ask, and it shall be given you; seek, and ye shall find; knock, and it shall be opened unto you. For every one that asketh receiveth; and he that seeketh findeth; and to him that knocketh it shall be opened.

"Or what man is there of you, whom if his son ask bread, will he give him a stone? Or if he ask a fish, will he give him a serpent? If ye then, being evil, know how to give good gifts unto your children, how much more shall your Father which is in heaven give good things to them that ask him?

"Therefore all things whatsoever ye would that men should do to you, do ye even so to them, for this is the law and the prophets.

"Whosoever heareth these sayings of mine and doeth them, I will liken him unto a wise man which built his house upon a rock. And the rain descended, and the floods came, and the winds blew, and beat upon that house. And it fell not, for it was founded upon a rock. And every one that heareth these sayings of mine and doeth them not shall be likened unto a foolish man which built his house upon the sand. And the rain descended, and the floods came, and the winds blew, and beat upon that house. And it fell, and great was the fall of it."

When Jesus had ended these sayings, the people were astonished at his doctrine, for he taught them as one having authority, and not as the scribes.

Now it came to pass on a certain day that he went into a ship with his disciples, and he said unto them, "Let us go over unto the other side of the lake." And they launched forth, and behold there arose a great tempest in the sea, insomuch that the ship was covered with waves; but he was asleep. And his disciples came to him and awoke him, saying, "Lord, save us! We perish!"

He saith unto them, "Why are ye fearful, O ye of little faith?" Then he arose and rebuked the winds

THE TRANSFIGURATION, by *FRA ANGELICO* (1387-1455)
The original is in San Marco, Florence.
Courtesy of Rudolph Lesch Fine Arts, Inc.

and the sea, and there was a great calm. But the men marvelled, saying, "What manner of man is this, that even the winds and the sea obey him!"

When he was come to the other side, there met him two possessed with devils, coming out of the tombs, exceeding fierce, so that no man might pass by that way. And behold they cried out, saying, "What have we to do with thee, Jesus, thou Son of God? Art thou come hither to torment us before the time?"

There was a good way off from them an herd of many swine feeding. So the devils besought him, saying, "If thou cast us out, suffer us to go away into the herd of swine." And he said unto them, "Go."

And when they were come out, they went into the herd of swine, and behold the whole herd of swine ran violently down a steep place into the sea, and perished in the waters. And they that kept them fled, and went their ways into the city and told every thing, and what was befallen to the possessed of the devils. And behold the whole city came out to meet

Jesus; and when they saw him, they besought him that he would depart out of their coasts.

And he entered into a ship and passed over, and came into his own city. And behold they brought to him a man sick of the palsy, lying on a bed. Jesus, seeing their faith, said unto the sick of the palsy, "Son, be of good cheer. Thy sins be forgiven thee."

Behold certain of the scribes said within themselves, "This man blasphemeth!" Jesus, knowing their thoughts, said:

"Wherefore think ye evil in your hearts? For whether is easier, to say 'Thy sins be forgiven thee,' or to say 'Arise, and walk'? But that ye may know that the Son of man hath power on earth to forgive sins" (then saith he to the sick of the palsy), "Arise, take up thy bed, and go unto thine house."

And he arose and departed to his house, but when the multitudes saw it, they marvelled and glorified God, which had given such power unto men.

As Jesus passed forth from thence he saw a man named Matthew sitting at the receipt of custom, and he saith unto him, "Follow me." And he arose and followed him.

It came to pass, as Jesus sat at meat in the house, behold many publicans and sinners came and sat down with him and his disciples. And when the Pharisees saw it, they said unto his disciples, "Why eateth your Master with publicans and sinners?" But when Jesus heard that, he said unto them: "They that be whole need not a physician, but they that are sick. For I am not come to call the righteous, but sinners, to repentance."

While he spake these things unto them, behold there came a certain ruler and worshipped him, saying, "My daughter is even now dead. But come and lay thy hand upon her, and she shall live." And Jesus arose and followed him, and so did his disciples. When Jesus came into the ruler's house and saw the minstrels and the people making a noise, he said unto them, "Give place, for the maid is not dead, but sleepeth." And they laughed him to scorn. But when the people were put forth, he went in and took her by the hand, and the maid arose. And the fame hereof went abroad into all that land.

When Jesus departed thence, two blind men followed him, crying and saying, "Thou Son of David, have mercy on us!" When he was come into the house, the blind men came to him, and Jesus saith unto them, "Believe ye that I am able to do this?" They said unto him, "Yea, Lord." Then touched he their eyes, saying, "According to your faith be it unto you." And their eyes were opened. Jesus straitly charged them, saying, "See that no man know it," but they, when they were departed, spread abroad his fame in all that country.

When he had called unto him his twelve disciples, he gave them power against unclean spirits, to cast them out, and to heal all manner of sickness and all manner of disease. Now the names of the twelve apostles are these: The first, Simon, who is called Peter, and Andrew his brother; James the son of Zebedee, and John his brother; Philip and Bartholomew; Thomas, and Matthew the publican; James the son of Alphaeus, and Lebbaeus, whose surname was Thaddaeus; Simon the Canaanite; and Judas Iscariot, who also betrayed him. These twelve Jesus sent forth and commanded them, saying:

"Go to the lost sheep of the house of Israel, and as ye go preach, saying, 'The kingdom of heaven is at hand.' Heal the sick, cleanse the lepers, raise the dead, cast out devils. Freely ye have received, freely give."

And they departed and went through the towns, preaching the gospel and healing everywhere. And the apostles, when they were returned, told him all that they had done, and he said unto them, "Come ye yourselves apart into a desert place and rest a while." For there were many coming and going, and they had no leisure so much as to eat. And they departed into a desert place by ship privately.

The people saw them departing, and many knew him, and ran afoot thither out of all cities and came together unto him. Jesus, when he came out, saw much people and was moved with compassion toward them because they were as sheep not having a shepherd, and he began to teach them many things.

When the day was now far spent, his disciples came unto him and said: "This is a desert place and now the time is far passed. Send them away, that they may go into the country round about and into the villages and buy themselves bread. For they have nothing to eat." He answered and said unto them, "Give ye them to eat." And they say unto him, "Shall we go and buy two hundred pennyworth of bread and give them to eat?" He saith unto them, "How many loaves have ye? Go and see." And when they knew, they say, "Five and two fishes." And he commanded them to make all sit down by companies upon the green grass, and they sat down in ranks, by hundreds and by fifties.

When he had taken the five loaves and the two fishes, he looked up to heaven and blessed and brake the loaves, and gave them to his disciples to set before them, and the two fishes divided he among them all. And they did all eat and were filled, and they took up twelve baskets full of the fragments and of the fishes. And they that did eat of the loaves were about five thousand men.

And straightway he constrained his disciples to get into the ship and to go to the other side, while he sent away the people. When he had sent the multitudes away, he went up into a mountain apart to pray. And when the evening was come, he was there alone.

But the ship was now in the midst of the sea, tossed with waves, for the wind was contrary. In the fourth watch of the night Jesus went unto them, walking on the sea. And when the disciples saw him walking on the sea, they were troubled, saying, "It is a spirit." And they cried out for fear. But straightway Jesus spake unto them, saying, "Be of good cheer, it is I. Be not afraid." Peter answered him and said, "Lord, if it be thou, bid me come unto thee on the water." He said, "Come."

When Peter was come down out of the ship, he walked on the water to go to Jesus. But when he saw the wind boisterous, he was afraid, and beginning to sink, he cried saying, "Lord, save me." And immediately Jesus stretched forth his hand and caught him, and said unto him, "O thou of little faith, wherefore didst thou doubt?" And when they were come into the ship, the wind ceased. Then they that were in the ship came and worshipped him, saying, "Of a truth thou art the Son of God."

When they were gone over, they came into the land of Gennesaret. And when the men of that place had knowledge of him, they sent out into all that country round about, and brought unto him all that were diseased, and besought him that they might only touch the hem of his garment, and as many as touched were made perfectly whole.

And they brought young children to him, that he should touch them. And his disciples rebuked those that brought them. But when Jesus saw it, he was much displeased and said unto them: "Suffer the little children to come unto me, and forbid them not, for of such is the kingdom of God. Verily I say unto you, whosoever shall not receive the kingdom of God as a little child, he shall not enter therein." And he took them up in his arms, put his hands upon them, and blessed them.

CHRIST ENTERING JERUSALEM, by *FRA ANGELICO*
(1387-1455)
The original is in San Marco, Florence.
Courtesy of Rudolph Lesch Fine Arts, Inc.

IV

IT came to pass about an eight days after these sayings he took Peter and John and James and went up into a mountain to pray. And as he prayed the fashion of his countenance was altered, and his raiment was white and glistering. And behold there talked with him two men, which were Moses and Elias, who appeared in glory and spake of his decease which he should accomplish at Jerusalem.

But Peter and they that were with him were heavy with sleep. When they were awake, they saw his glory and the two men that stood with him. And it came to pass as they departed from him, Peter said unto Jesus: "Master, it is good for us to be here. And let us make three tabernacles, one for thee, and one for Moses, and one for Elias"—not knowing what he said.

While he thus spake, there came a cloud and overshadowed them, and they feared as they entered into the cloud. And there came a voice out of the cloud, saying: "This is my beloved Son. Hear him." When the voice was past, Jesus was found alone. And they kept it close, and told no man in those days any of those things which they had seen.

Now the feast of unleavened bread drew nigh which is called the Passover. Jesus, going up to Jerusalem, took the twelve disciples apart in the way and said unto them:

"Behold we go up to Jerusalem. And the Son of man shall be betrayed unto the chief priests and unto the scribes, and they shall condemn him to death, and shall deliver him to the Gentiles to mock, and to scourge, and to crucify him. And the third day he shall rise again."

When they drew nigh unto Jerusalem and were come to Bethphage, unto the mount of Olives, then sent Jesus two disciples, saying unto them:

"Go into the villáge over against you, and straightway ye shall find an ass tied and a colt with her. Loose them and bring them unto me. And if any man say ought unto you, ye shall say, 'The Lord hath need of them,' and straightway he will send them."

The disciples went and did as Jesus commanded them, and brought the ass and the colt, and put on them their clothes, and they set him thereon. And a very great multitude spread their garments in the way. Others cut down branches from the trees and strawed them in the way. And the multitudes that went before and that followed cried, saying:

"Hosanna to the son of David! Blessed is he that cometh in the name of the Lord! Hosanna in the highest!"

When he was come into Jerusalem, all the city was moved, saying, "Who is this?" And the multitude said, "This is Jesus the prophet of Nazareth of Galilee." And Jesus went into the temple of God and cast out all them that sold and bought in the temple, and overthrew the tables of the moneychangers and the seats of them that sold doves, and said unto them, "It is written 'My house shall be called the house of prayer,' but ye have made it a den of thieves." And the blind and the lame came to him in the temple, and he healed them.

And he taught daily in the temple. But the chief priests and the scribes and the chief of the people sought to destroy him, and could not find what they might do, for all the people were very attentive to hear him. Then went the Pharisees and took counsel how they might entangle him in his talk. And they sent out unto him their disciples, saying:

"Master, we know that thou art true and teachest the way of God in truth. Tell us therefore: What thinkest thou, is it lawful to give tribute unto Caesar or not?"

But Jesus perceived their wickedness and said, "Why tempt ye me, ye hypocrites? Shew me the tribute money." And they brought unto him a penny. He saith unto them, "Whose is this image and superscription?" They say unto him, "Caesar's." Then saith he unto them, "Render therefore unto Caesar the things which are Caesar's, and unto God the things that are God's." When they had heard these words, they marvelled, and left him and went their way.

Then assembled together the chief priests and the scribes and the elders of the people unto the palace of the high priest, who was called Caiaphas, and consulted that they might take Jesus by subtilty and kill him. But they said, "Not on the feast day, lest there be an uproar among the people."

Now when Jesus was in Bethany in the house of Simon the leper, there came unto him a woman having an alabaster box of very precious ointment, and poured it on his head as he sat at meat. But when his disciples saw it, they had indignation, saying, "To what purpose is this waste? For this ointment might have been sold for much and given to the poor." When Jesus understood it, he said unto them:

"Why trouble ye the woman? For she hath wrought a good work upon me. For ye have the poor always with you, but me ye have not always. For in that she hath poured this ointment on my body, she did it for

THE TRIBUTE MONEY, by TITIAN (1477-1576)
The original is in the Dresden Gallery, Dresden.
Courtesy of Rudolph Lesch Fine Arts, Inc.

my burial. Verily I say unto you, wheresoever this gospel shall be preached in the whole world, there shall also this that this woman hath done be told for a memorial of her."

Then one of the twelve, called Judas Iscariot, went unto the chief priests and said unto them, "What will ye give me, and I will deliver him unto you?" And they covenanted with him for thirty pieces of silver, and from that time he sought opportunity to betray him.

Now the first day of the feast of unleavened bread the disciples came to Jesus, saying unto him, "Where wilt thou that we prepare for thee to eat the passover?" He said, "Go into the city to such a man and say unto him, 'The Master saith, "My time is at hand. I will keep the passover at thy house with my disciples."'" The disciples did as Jesus had appointed them, and they made ready the passover.

Now when the even was come, he sat down with the twelve. And as they did eat, he said, "Verily I say unto you that one of you shall betray me." And they were exceeding sorrowful and began every one of them to say unto him, "Lord, is it I?" Then Judas, which betrayed him, answered and said, "Master, is it I?" He said unto him, "Thou hast said."

And as they were eating, Jesus took bread and blessed it and brake it, and gave it to the disciples, and said, "Take, eat; this is my body." And he took the cup, and gave thanks, and gave it to them, saying, "Drink ye all of it, for this is my blood of the new testament, which is shed for many for the remission of sins. But I say unto you, I will not drink henceforth of this fruit of the vine until that day when I drink it new with you in my Father's kingdom."

When they had sung an hymn, they went out into the mount of Olives. Then saith Jesus unto them: "All ye shall be offended because of me this night. For it is written, 'I will smite the shepherd, and the sheep of the flock shall be scattered abroad.' But after I am risen again, I will go before you into Galilee."

Peter answered and said unto him, "Though all

men shall be offended because of thee, yet will I never be offended." Jesus said unto him, "Verily I say unto thee that this night, before the cock crow, thou shalt deny me thrice." Peter said unto him, "Though I should die with thee, yet will I not deny thee." Likewise also said all the disciples.

Then cometh Jesus with them unto a place called Gethsemane, and saith unto the disciples, "Sit ye here while I go and pray yonder." And he took with him Peter and the two sons of Zebedee, and began to be sorrowful and very heavy. Then saith he unto them: "My soul is exceeding sorrowful, even unto death. Tarry ye here and watch with me."

He went a little farther, and fell on his face, and prayed, saying, "O my Father, if it be possible, let this cup pass from me. Nevertheless not as I will, but as thou wilt." And he cometh unto the disciples and findeth them asleep, and saith unto Peter: "What! Could ye not watch with me onè hour? Watch and pray, that ye enter not into temptation. The spirit indeed is willing, but the flesh is weak."

He went away again the second time and prayed, saying, "O my Father, if this cup may not pass away from me except I drink it, thy will be done." And he came and found them asleep again, for their eyes were heavy. And he left them and went away again, and prayed the third time saying the same words. Then cometh he to his disciples and saith unto them: "Behold the hour is at hand, and the Son of man is betrayed into the hands of sinners. Rise, let us be going. Behold he is at hand that doth betray me."

While he yet spake, lo, Judas, one of the twelve, came, and with him a great multitude with swords and staves, from the chief priests and elders of the people. Now he that betrayed him gave them a sign, saying: "Whomsoever I shall kiss, that same is he. Hold him fast." And forthwith he came to Jesus and said, "Hail, Master!" and kissed him. Jesus said unto him, "Friend, wherefore art thou come?"

Then came they and laid hands on Jesus, and took him. And behold, one of them which were with Jesus stretched out his hand, and drew his sword, and struck a servant of the high priest's, and smote off his ear. Then said Jesus unto him, "Put up again thy sword into his place, for all they that take the sword shall perish with the sword." And he touched his ear and healed him.

Then Jesus said unto the chief priests and captains of the temple and the elders, which were come to him: "Be ye come out as against a thief with swords and staves? When I was daily with you in the temple ye stretched forth no hands against me. But this is your hour and the power of darkness."

They that had laid hold on Jesus led him away to Caiaphas, the high priest, where the scribes and the elders were assembled. Then all the disciples forsook him and fled. But Peter followed him afar off unto the high priest's palace, and went in and sat with the servants, to see the end. And when they had kindled a fire in the midst of the hall and were set down together, Peter sat down among them. But a certain maid beheld him as he sat by the fire, and earnestly looked upon him, and said, "This man was also with

THE LAST SUPPER, by *LEONARDO DA VINCI* (1452-1519)
The original is in the Refectory of Santa Maria delle Grazie, Milan.
Courtesy of Rudolph Lesch Fine Arts, Inc.

him." And he denied him, saying, "Woman, I know him not." After a little while another saw him and said, "Thou art also of them." And Peter said, "Man, I am not." About the space of one hour after, another confidently affirmed, saying, "Of a truth this fellow also was with him, for he is a Galilaean." And Peter said, "Man, I know not what thou sayest." Immediately, while he yet spake, the cock crew. And the Lord turned and looked upon Peter. And Peter went out and wept bitterly.

Now the chief priests and elders and all the council sought false witness against Jesus, to put him to death, but found none. Yea, though many false witnesses came, yet found they none. At the last came two false witnesses and said, "This fellow said, 'I am able to destroy the temple of God and to build it in three days.'"

The high priest arose and said unto him, "Answerest thou nothing? What is it which these witness against thee?" But Jesus held his peace. And the high priest said unto him, "I adjure thee by the living God that thou tell us whether thou be the Christ, the Son of God."

Jesus saith unto him: "Thou hast said. Nevertheless I say unto you, hereafter shall ye see the Son of man sitting on the right hand of power, and coming in the clouds of heaven."

Then the high priest rent his clothes, saying: "He hath spoken blasphemy. What further need have we of witnesses? Behold, now ye have heard his blasphemy. What think ye?"

They answered and said, "He is guilty of death."

V

WHEN the morning was come, all the chief priests and elders of the people took counsel against Jesus to put him to death. And when they had bound him, they led him away and delivered him to Pontius Pilate, the governor.

Then Judas, which had betrayed him, when he saw that he was condemned, repented himself, and brought again the thirty pieces of silver to the chief priests and elders, saying, "I have sinned in that I have betrayed the innocent blood." They said: "What is that to us? See thou to that." And he cast down the pieces of silver in the temple, and departed, and went and hanged himself. The chief priests took the silver pieces and said, "It is not lawful for to put them in the treasury, because it is the price of blood." And they took counsel, and bought with them the potter's field to bury strangers in. Wherefore that field was called the field of blood unto this day.

Jesus stood before the governor. And the whole multitude began to accuse him, saying, "We found this fellow perverting the nation, saying that he himself is Christ, a King." Pilate asked him, saying, "Art thou the King of the Jews?" And he answered him and said, "Thou sayest it."

Then said Pilate to the chief priests and to the people, "I find no fault in this man." And they were the more fierce, saying, "He stirreth up the people, teaching throughout all Jewry." And when he was accused of the chief priests and elders, he answered nothing. Then said Pilate unto him, "Hearest thou not how many things they witness against thee?" And he answered him to never a word, insomuch that the governor marvelled greatly.

Now at that feast the governor was wont to release unto the people a prisoner, whom they would. They had then a notable prisoner called Barabbas. Therefore when they were gathered together, Pilate said unto them: "Whom will ye that I release unto you?

Barabbas, or Jesus which is called Christ?" For he knew that for envy they had delivered him.

When he was set down on the judgment seat, his wife sent unto him, saying, "Have thou nothing to do with that just man, for I have suffered many things this day in a dream because of him."

But the chief priests and elders persuaded the multitude that they should ask Barabbas and destroy Jesus. The governor answered and said unto them, "Whether of the twain will ye that I release unto you?" They said, "Barabbas!" Pilate saith unto them, "What shall I do then with Jesus, which is called Christ?" They all say unto him, "Let him be crucified!" The governor said, "Why, what evil hath he done?" But they cried out the more, saying, "Let him be crucified!"

When Pilate saw that he could prevail nothing, but that rather a tumult was made, he took water and washed his hands before the multitude, saying: "I am innocent of the blood of this just person. See ye to it." Then answered all the people and said, "His

BEHOLD THE MAN, by ANTONIO CISERI (1821-1891)
The original is in the Gallery of Modern Art, Florence.
Courtesy of Rudolph Lesch Fine Arts, Inc.

blood be on us and on our children."

Then released he Barabbas unto them. And when he had scourged Jesus, he delivered him to be crucified. Then the soldiers of the governor took Jesus into the common hall and gathered unto him the whole band of soldiers. And they stripped him and put on him a scarlet robe, and when they had platted a crown of thorns, they put it upon his head, and a reed in his right hand. And they bowed the knee before him and mocked him, saying, "Hail, King of the Jews!" And they spit upon him, and took the reed and smote him on the head.

After that they had mocked him, they took the robe off from him, and put his own raiment on him, and led him away to crucify him. And as they came out, they found a man of Cyrene, Simon by name. Him they compelled to bear his cross.

When they were come unto a place called Golgotha, that is to say, a place of a skull, they gave him vinegar to drink, mingled with gall; and when he had tasted thereof, he would not drink. And they crucified him, and parted his garments, casting lots. And sitting down, they watched him there; and set up over his head his accusation written "This is Jesus the King of the Jews."

And they that passed by reviled him, wagging their heads and saying, "Thou that destroyest the temple and buildest it in three days, save thyself. If thou be the Son of God, come down from the cross." Likewise also the chief priests mocking him, with the scribes and elders, said:

"He saved others; himself he cannot save. If he be the King of Israel, let him now come down from the cross and we will believe him. He trusted in God; let him deliver him now, if he will have him. For he said, 'I am the Son of God.'"

Then said Jesus, "Father, forgive them, for they know not what they do."

Then were there two thieves crucified with him, one on the right hand and another on the left. One of the malefactors which were hanged railed on him, saying, "If thou be Christ, save thyself and us." But the other answering rebuked him, saying: "Dost thou not fear God, seeing thou art in the same condemnation? And we indeed justly, for we receive the due reward of our deeds. But this man hath done nothing amiss." And he said unto Jesus, "Lord, remember me when thou comest into thy kingdom." Jesus said unto him, "Verily I say unto thee, today shalt thou be with me in paradise."

Now there stood by the cross of Jesus his mother, and his mother's sister, Mary the wife of Cleophas, and Mary Magdalene. When Jesus therefore saw his mother and the disciple standing by, whom he loved, he saith unto his mother, "Woman, behold thy son!" Then saith he to the disciple, "Behold thy mother!" And from that hour that disciple took her unto his own home.

Now from the sixth hour there was darkness over all the land unto the ninth hour. And about the ninth hour Jesus cried with a loud voice, saying, "*Eli, Eli, lama sabachthani?*" That is to say, "My God, my God, why hast thou forsaken me?" Some of them

THE CRUCIFIXION, by *FRA ANGELICO* (1387-1455)
The original is in San Marco, Florence.
Courtesy of Rudolph Lesch Fine Arts, Inc.

that stood there, when they heard that, said, "This man calleth for Elias."

Jesus, knowing that all things were now accomplished that the scripture might be fulfilled, saith, "I thirst." And straightway one of them ran, and took a sponge and filled it with vinegar, and put it on a reed, and gave him to drink. The rest said, "Let be. Let us see whether Elias will come to save him."

When Jesus therefore had received the vinegar, he said, "It is finished." And he bowed his head. And when Jesus had cried with a loud voice, he said, "Father, into thy hands I commend my spirit." And having said thus, he gave up the ghost.

And behold, the veil of the temple was rent in twain from the top to the bottom; and the earth did quake, and the rocks rent. The graves were opened, and many bodies of the saints which slept arose, and came out of the graves after his resurrection, and went into the holy city and appeared unto many. Now when they that were watching Jesus saw the earthquake and those things that were done, they feared greatly, saying, "Truly this was the Son of God."

When the even was come, there came a rich man of Arimathaea named Joseph, who also himself was Jesus' disciple. He went to Pilate and begged the body of Jesus. Then Pilate commanded the body to be delivered. When Joseph had taken the body, he wrapped it in a clean linen cloth, and laid it in his own new tomb which he had hewn out in the rock. And he rolled a great stone to the door of the sepulchre, and departed.

Now the next day the chief priests and Pharisees came together unto Pilate, saying: "Sir, we remember that that deceiver said while he was yet alive, 'After three days I will rise again.' Command therefore that the sepulchre be made sure until the third day, lest his disciples come by night and steal him away, and say unto the people, 'He is risen from the dead.' So the last error shall be worse than the first." Pilate said unto them, "Ye have a watch. Go your way; make it as sure as ye can." So they went and made the sepulchre sure, sealing the stone and setting a watch.

The first day of the week cometh Mary Magdalene early, when it was yet dark, unto the sepulchre, and seeth the stone taken away from the sepulchre. Then she runneth and cometh to Simon Peter and to the other disciple, whom Jesus loved, and saith unto them, "They have taken away the Lord out of the sepulchre, and we know not where they have laid him."

Peter therefore went forth and that other disciple, and came to the sepulchre. So they ran both together, and the other disciple did outrun Peter and came first to the sepulchre. And he, stooping down and looking in, saw the linen clothes lying. Yet went he not in. Then cometh Simon Peter, following him, and went into the sepulchre and seeth the linen clothes lie, and the napkin that was about his head, not lying with the linen clothes but wrapped together in a place by itself. Then went in also that other disciple, which came first to the sepulchre, and he saw and believed. Then the disciples went away again unto their own home.

But Mary stood without at the sepulchre weeping. And as she wept, she stooped down and looked into the sepulchre, and seeth two angels in white sitting, the one at the head and the other at the feet, where the body of Jesus had lain.

They say unto her, "Woman, why weepest thou?"

She saith unto them, "Because they have taken away my Lord and I know not where they have laid him."

When she had thus said, she turned herself back and saw Jesus standing, and knew not that it was Jesus.

Jesus saith unto her: "Woman, why weepest thou? Whom seekest thou?"

She, supposing him to be the gardener, saith unto him, "Sir, if thou have borne him hence, tell me where thou hast laid him, and I will take him away."

Jesus saith unto her, "Mary."

She turned herself and saith unto him, "*Rabboni,*"

which is to say, "Master."

Jesus saith unto her: "Touch me not, for I am not yet ascended to my Father. But go to my brethren and say unto them I ascend unto my Father and your Father, and to my God and your God." Mary Magdalene came and told the disciples that she had seen the Lord and that he had spoken these things unto her.

Now behold some of the watch came into the city and showed unto the chief priests all the things that were done. And when they were assembled with the elders and had taken counsel, they gave large money unto the soldiers, saying: "Say ye, 'His disciples came by night and stole him away while we slept.' And if this come to the governor's ears, we will persuade him and secure you." So they took the money and did as they were taught, and this saying is commonly reported among the Jews until this day.

Then the eleven disciples went away into Galilee, into a mountain where Jesus had appointed them. And when they saw him, they worshipped him. But

JESUS APPEARS TO MARY MAGDALENE, by *FRA ANGELICO*
(1387-1455)
The original is in San Marco, Florence.

some doubted. And Jesus came and spake unto them, saying:

"All power is given unto me in heaven and in earth. Go ye therefore and teach all nations, baptizing them in the name of the Father, and of the Son, and of the Holy Ghost; teaching them to observe all things whatsoever I have commanded you.

"And lo, I am with you alway, even unto the end of the world."